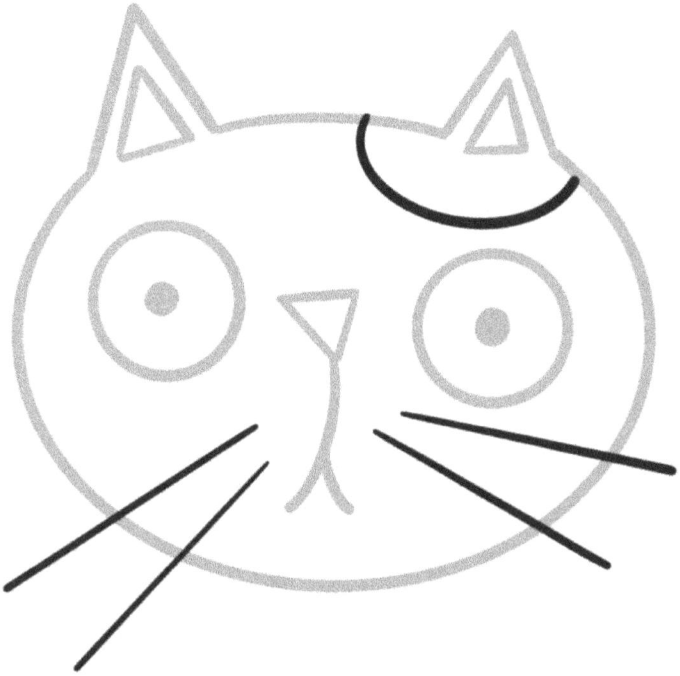

These cats belong to

....

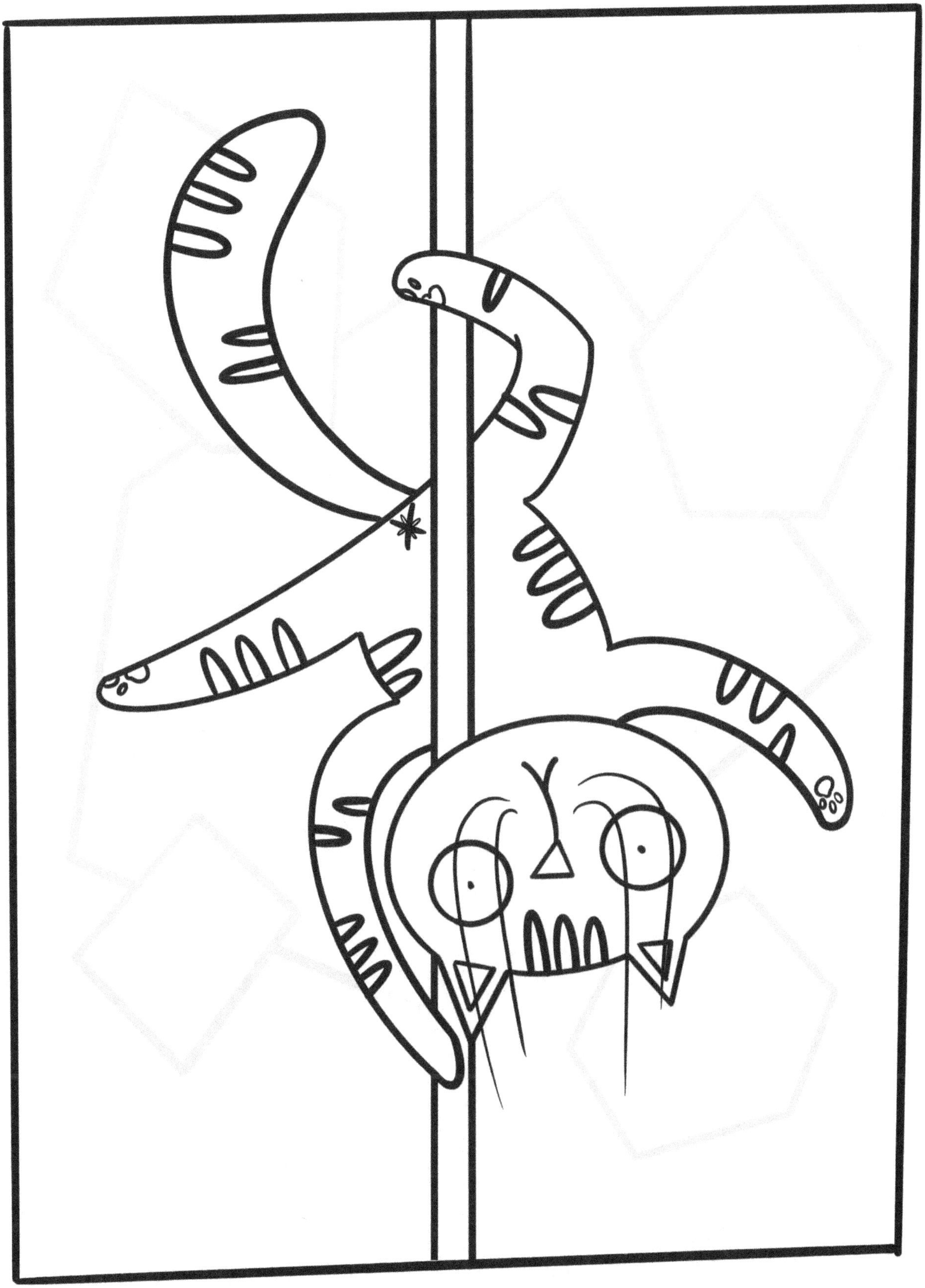

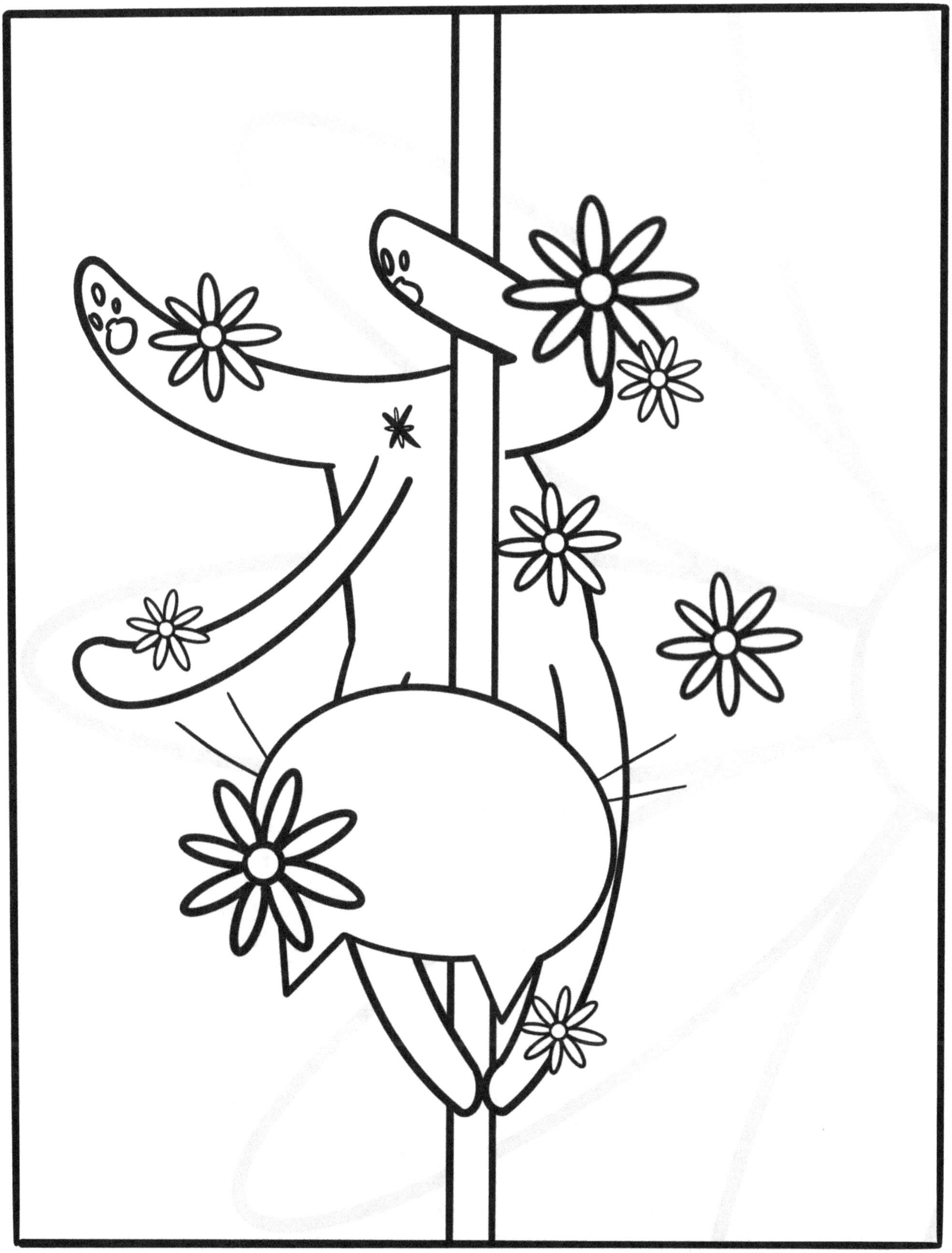

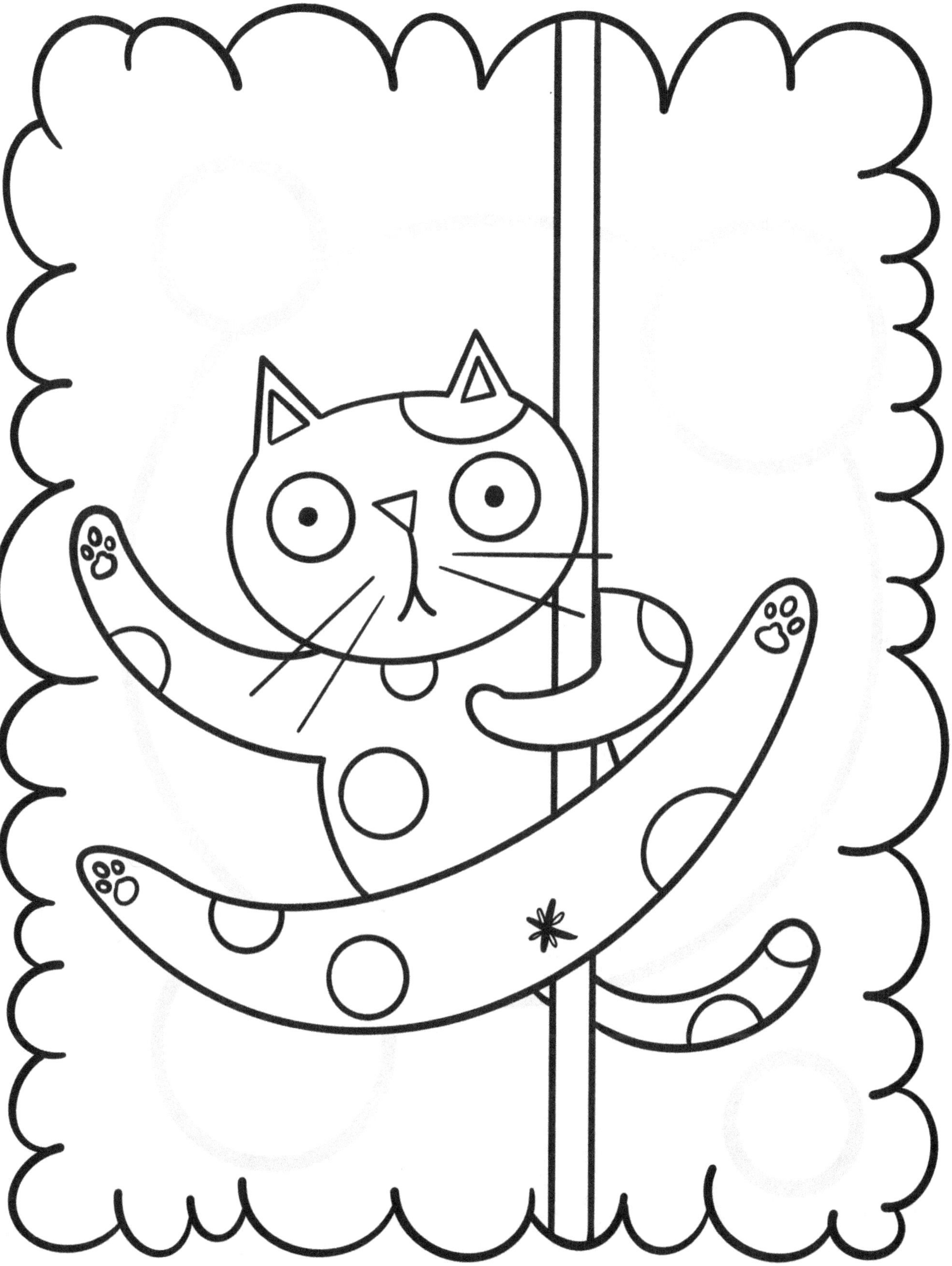

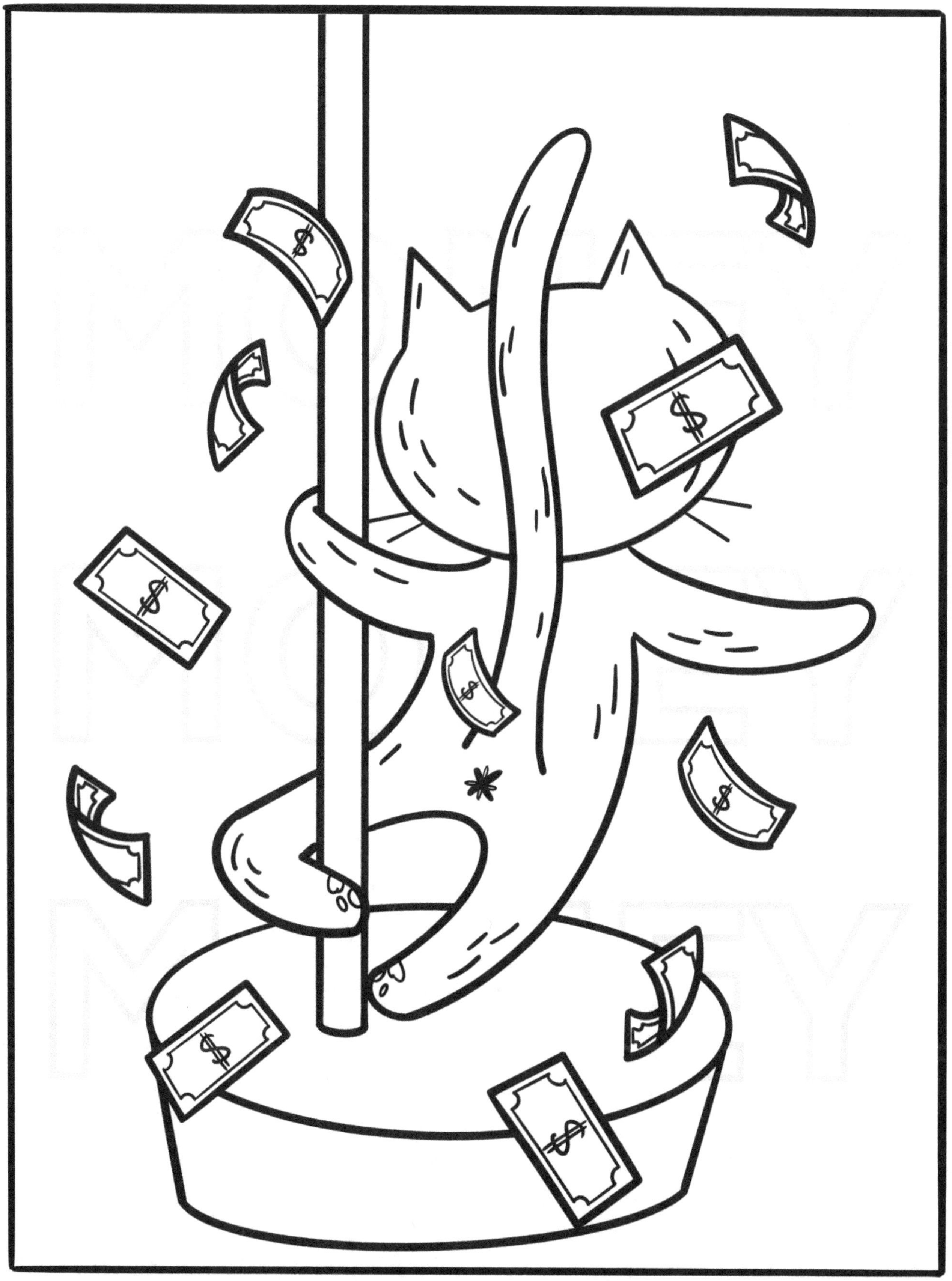

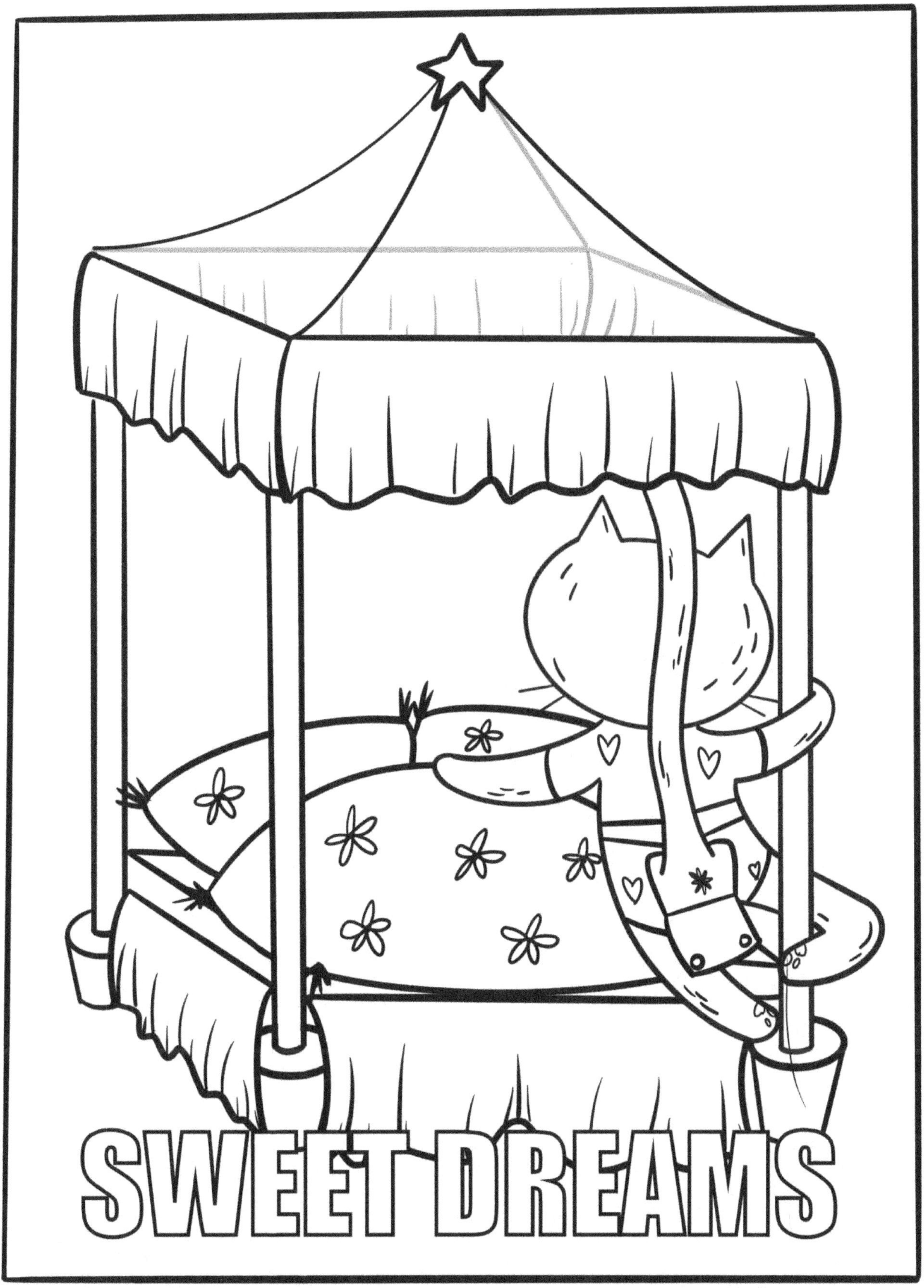
SWEET DREAMS

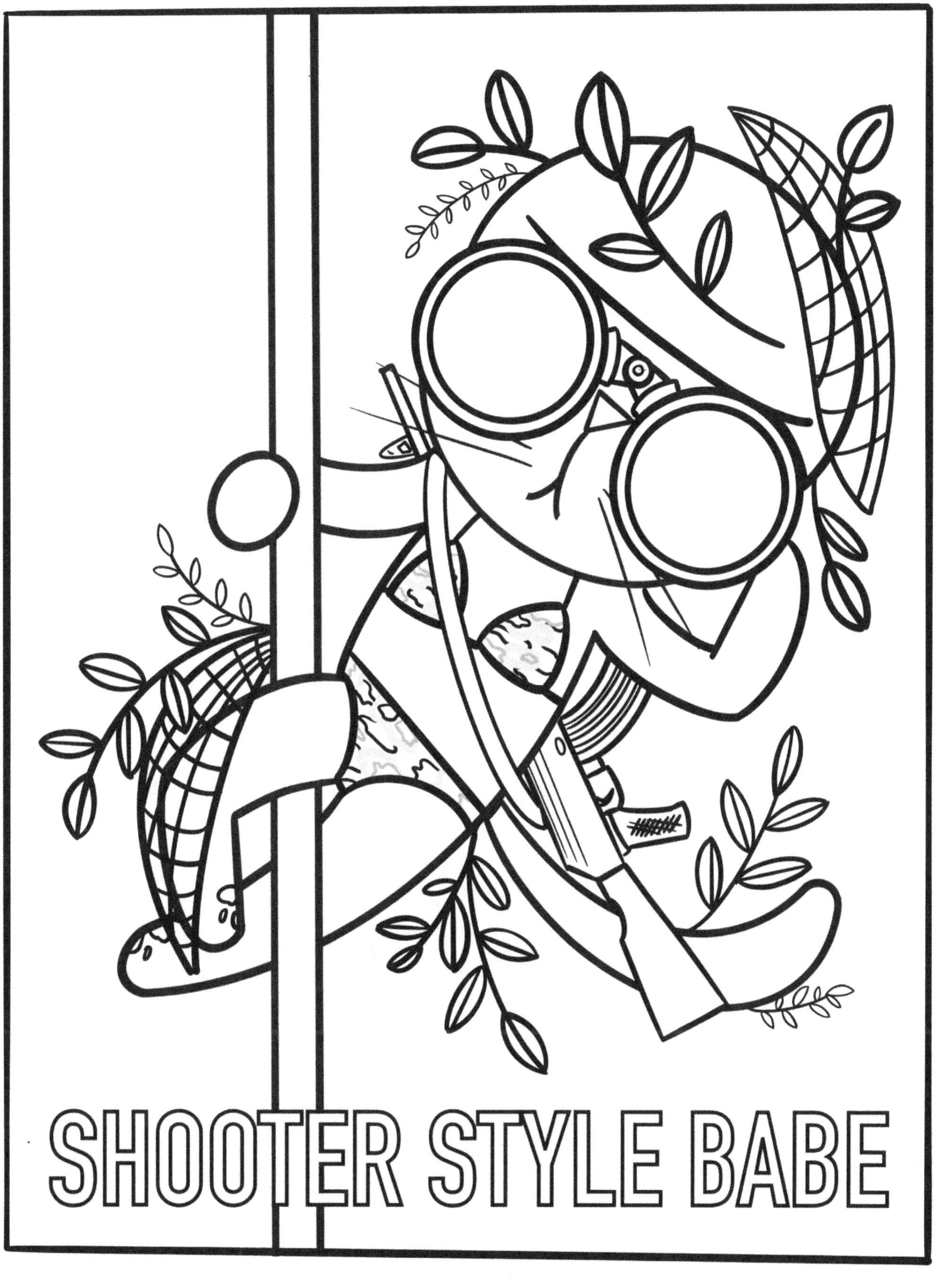
SHOOTER STYLE BABE

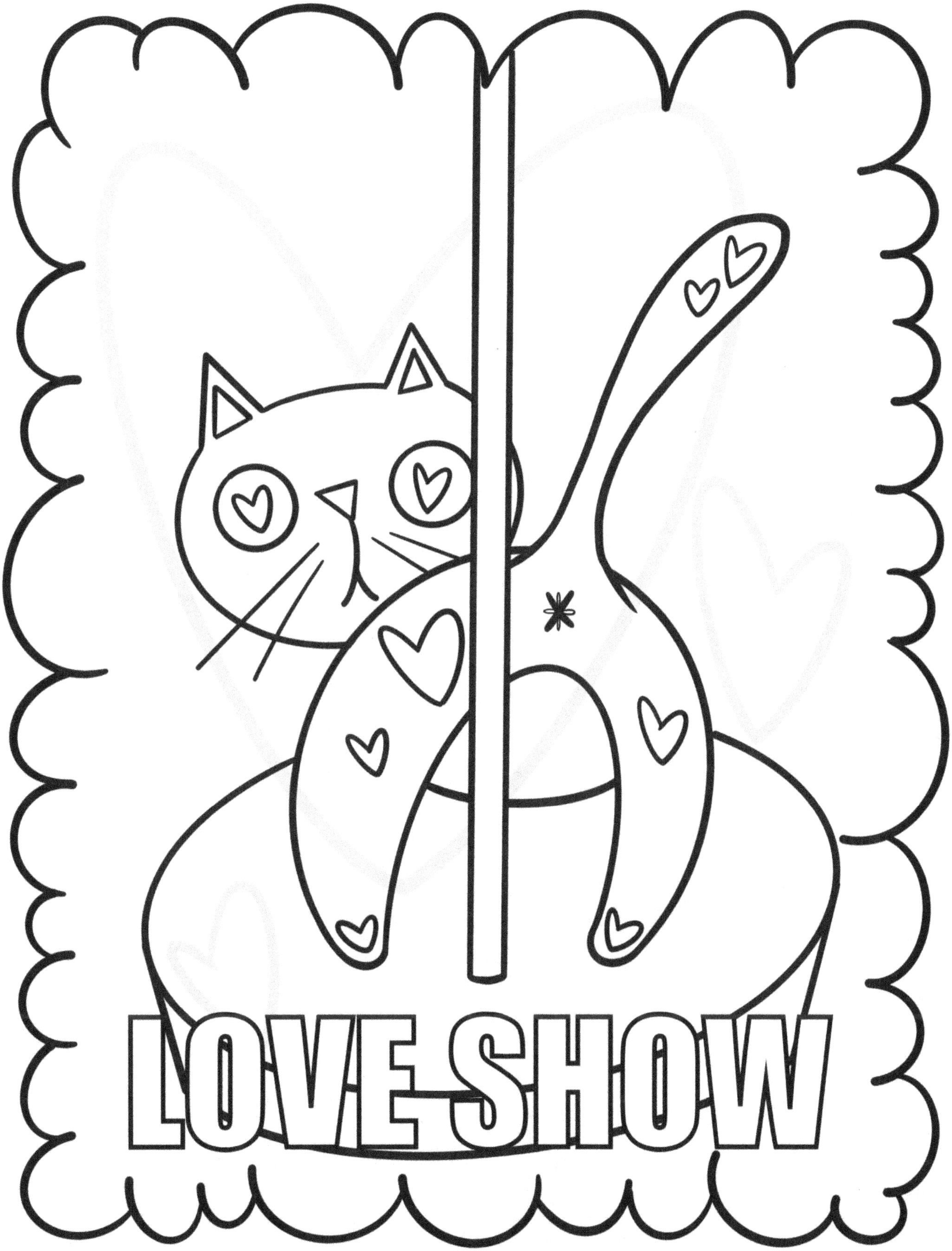
LOVE SHOW

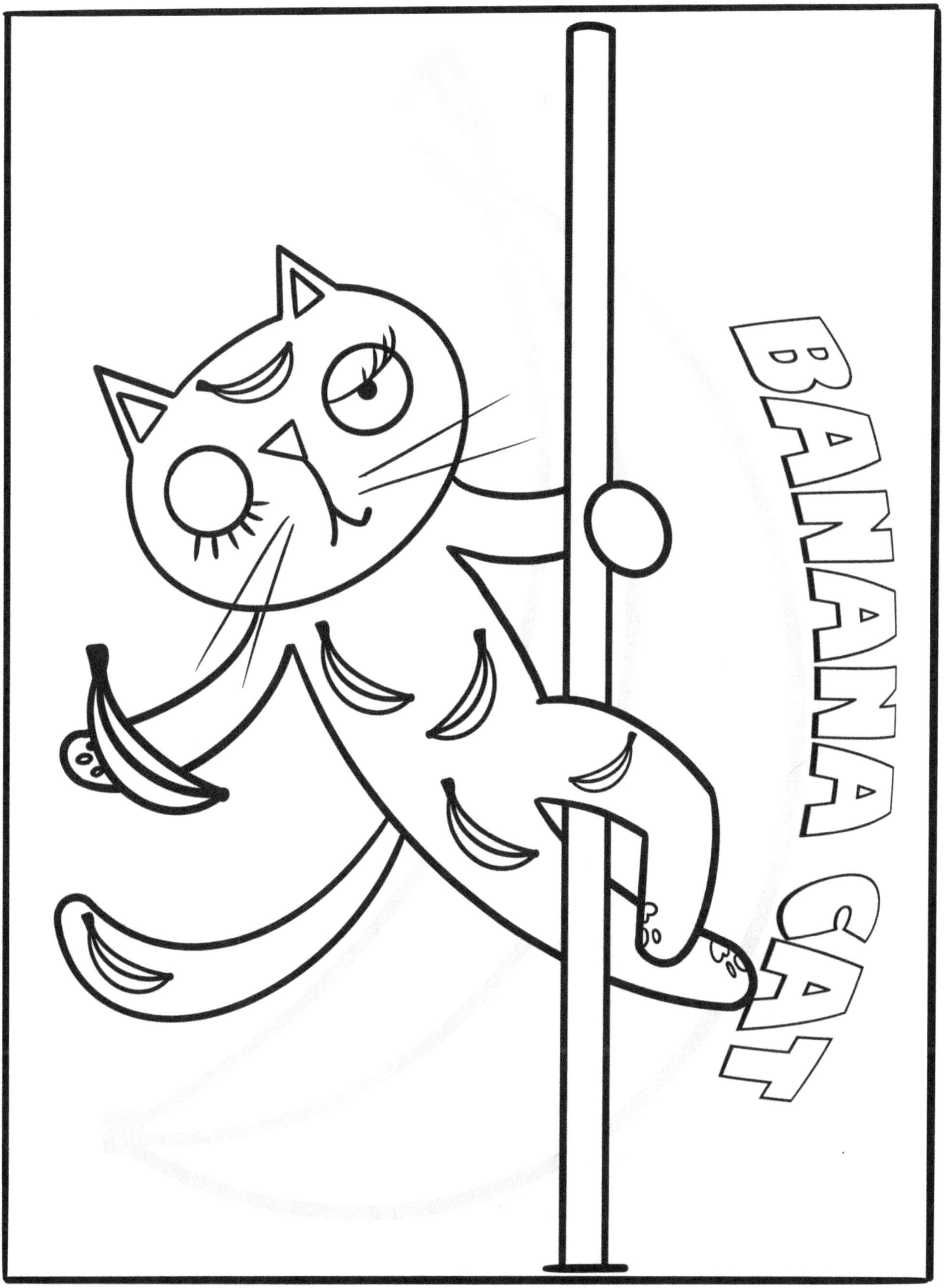
BANANA CAT

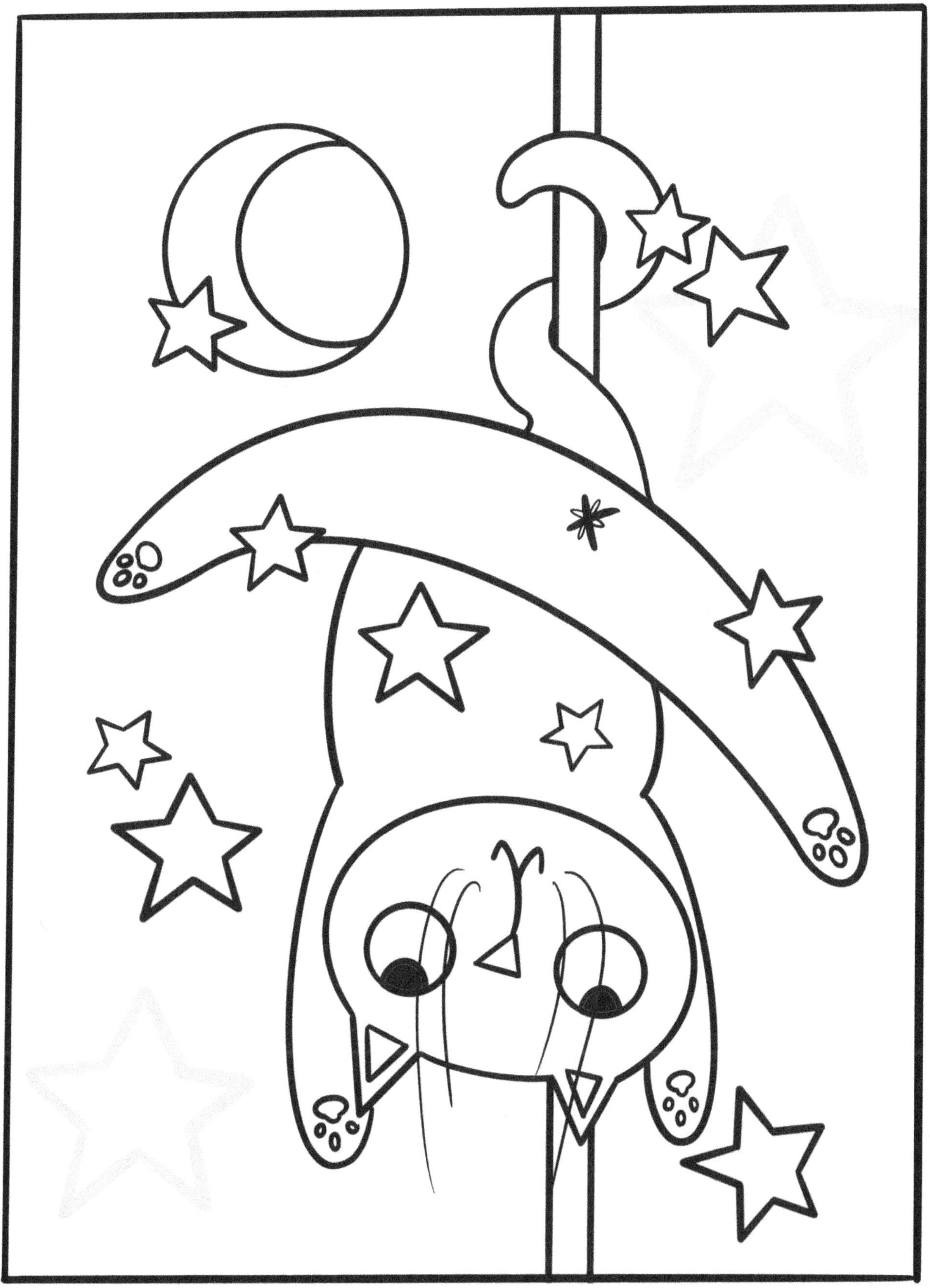

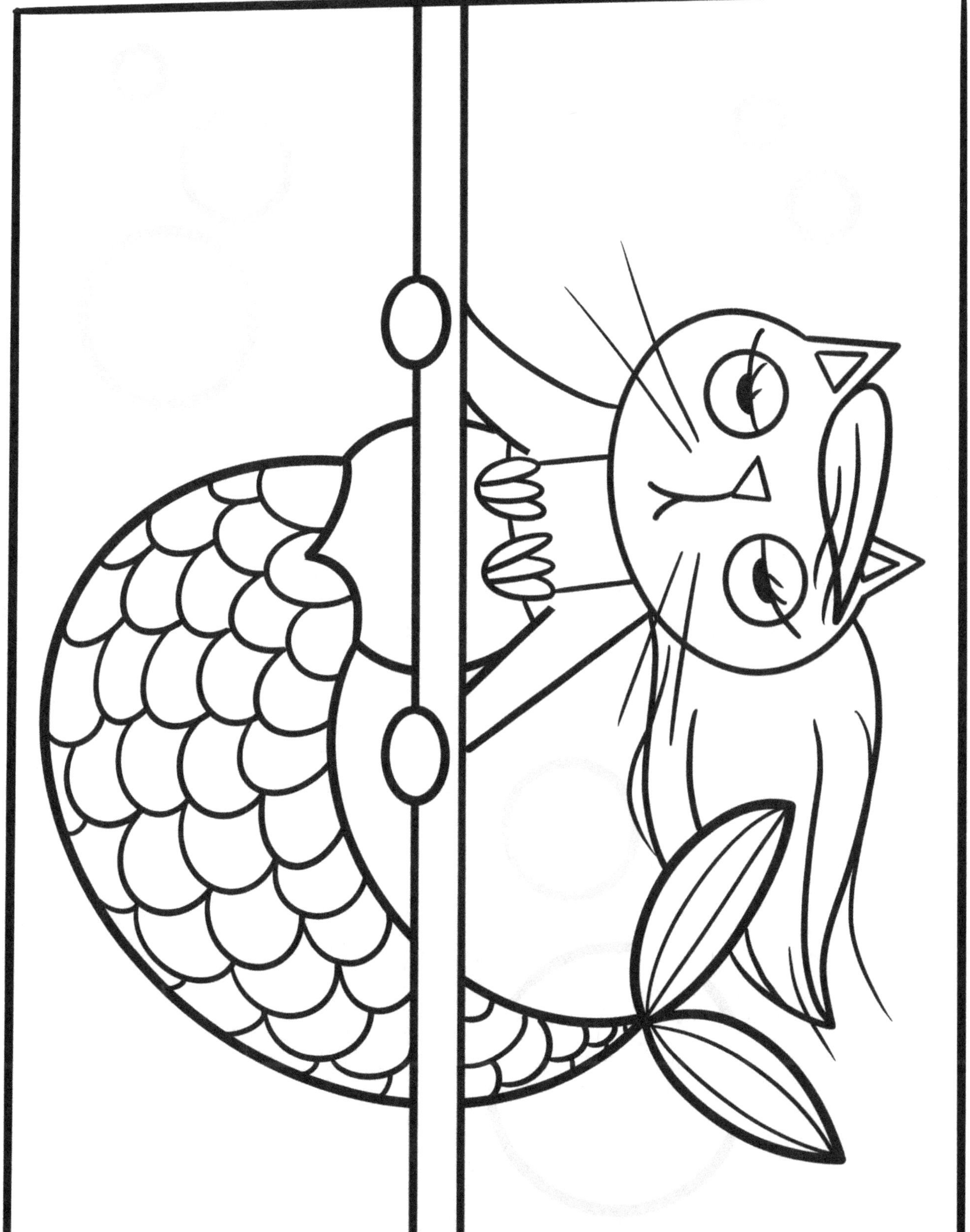

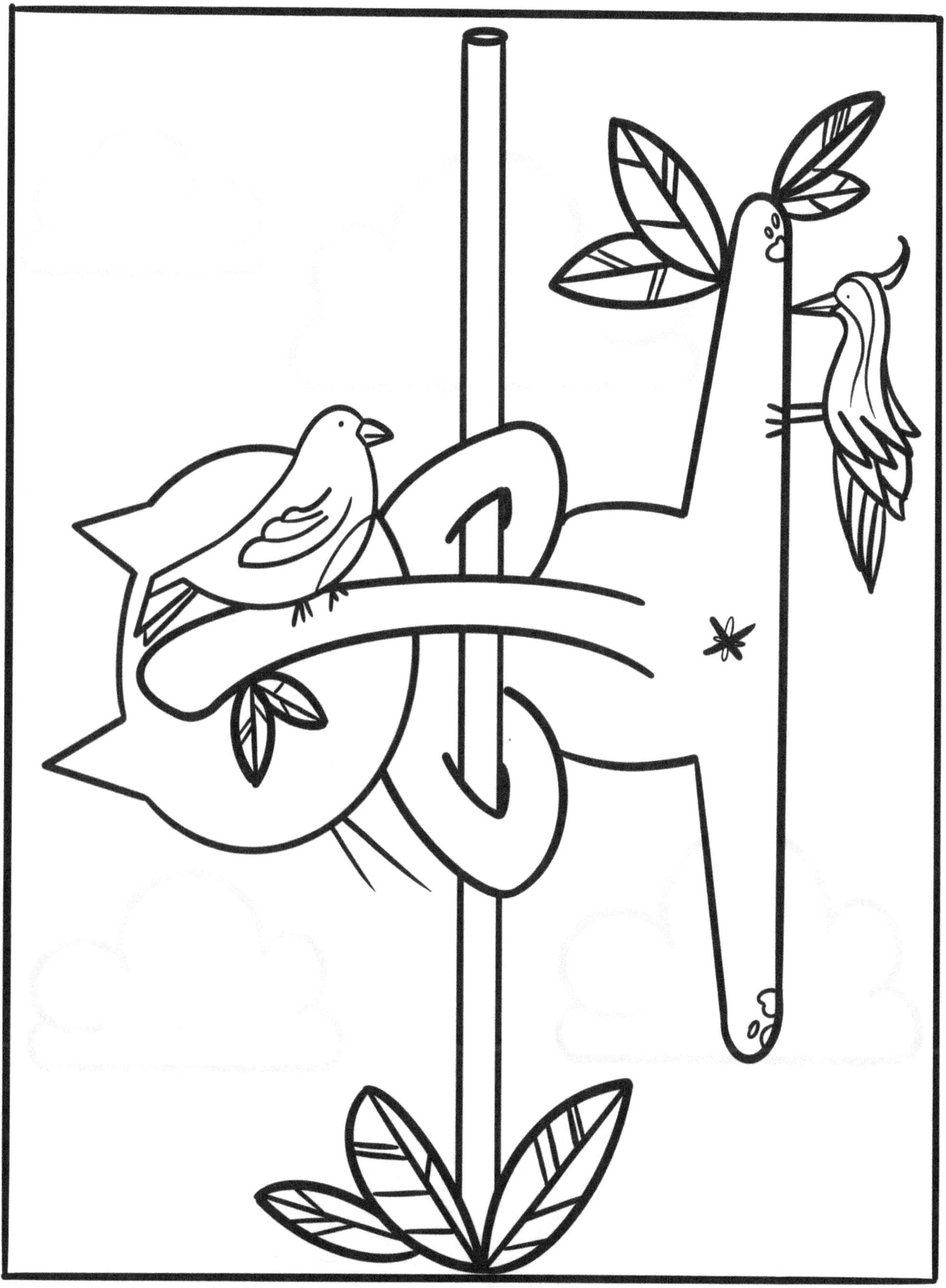

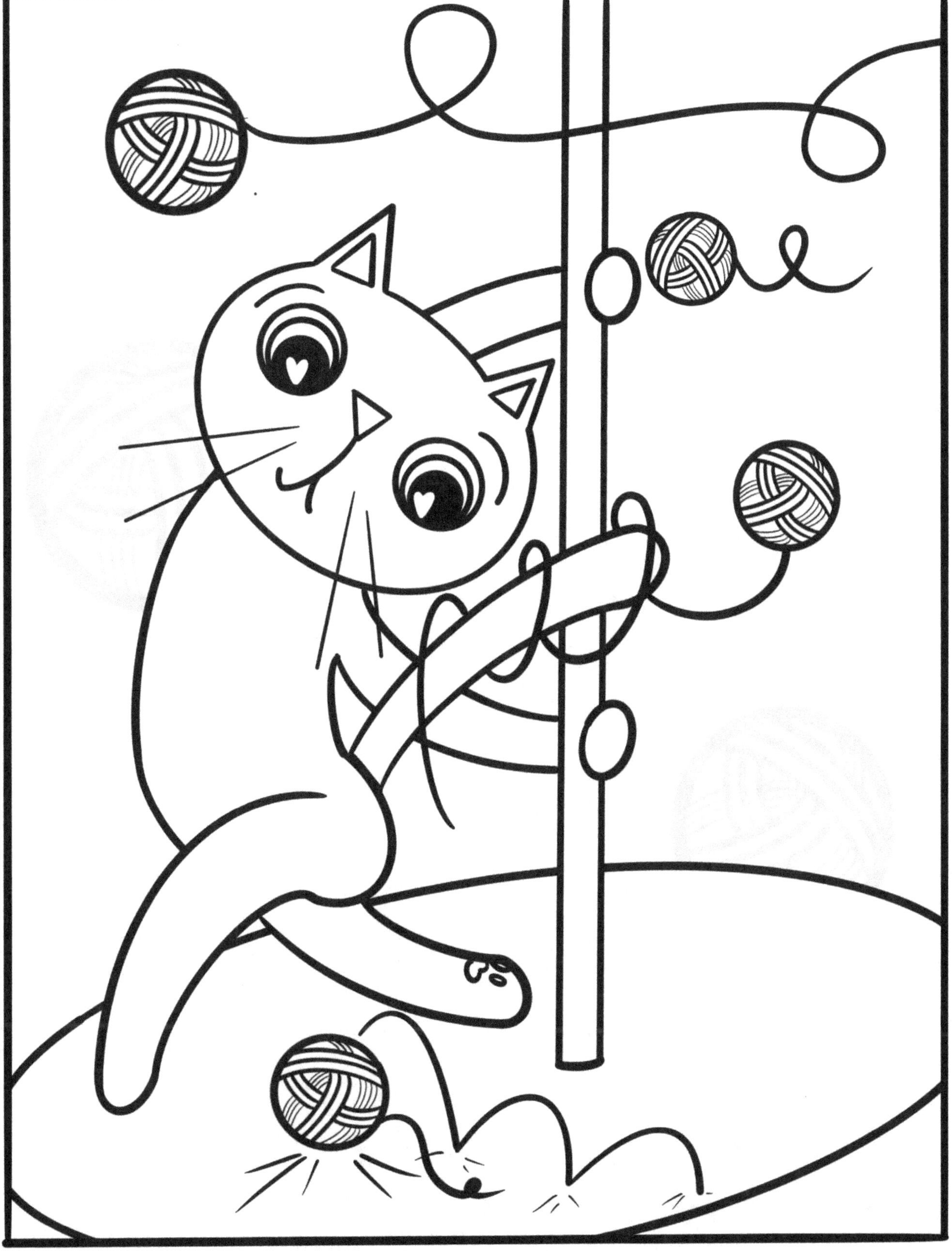

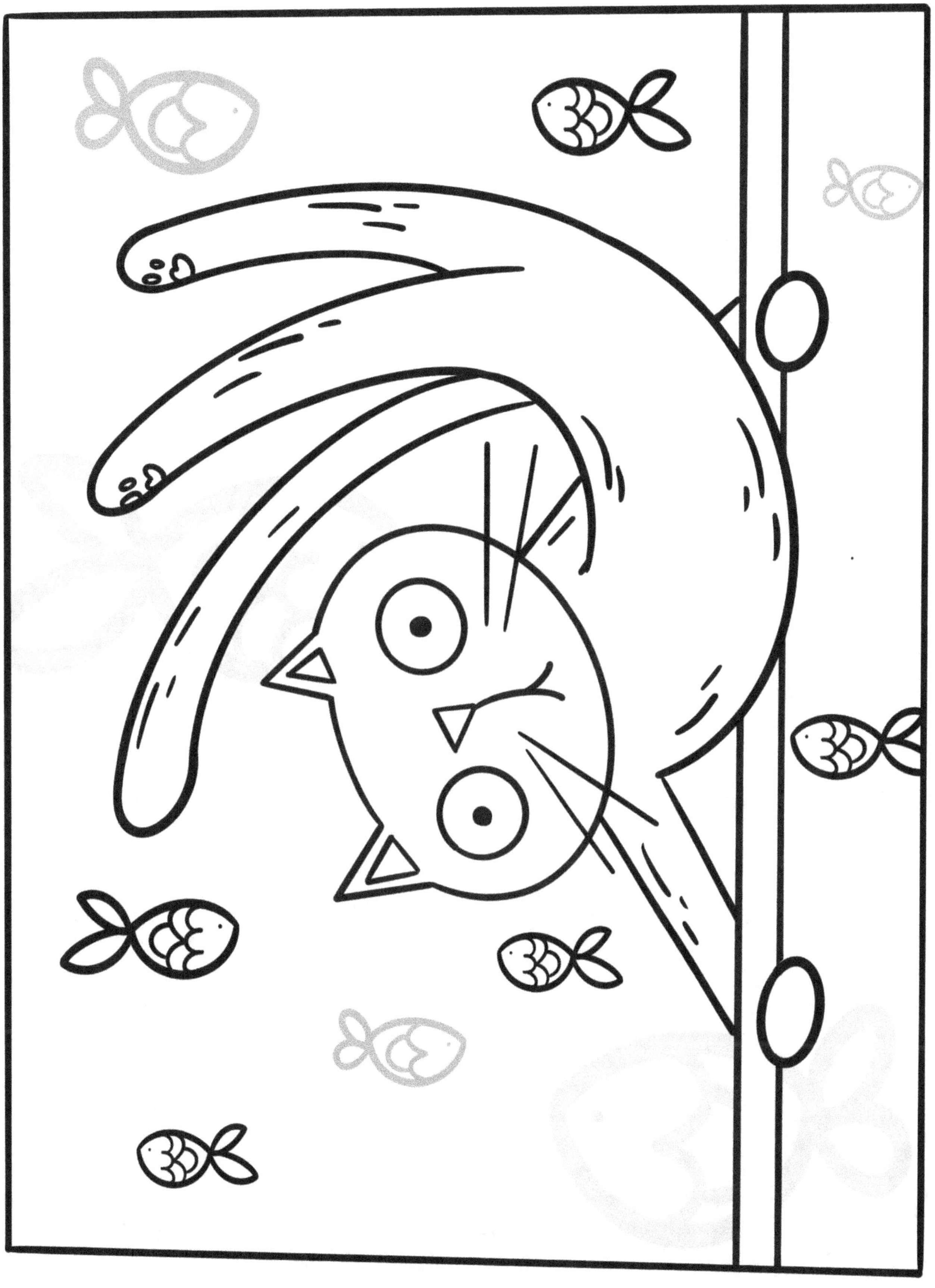

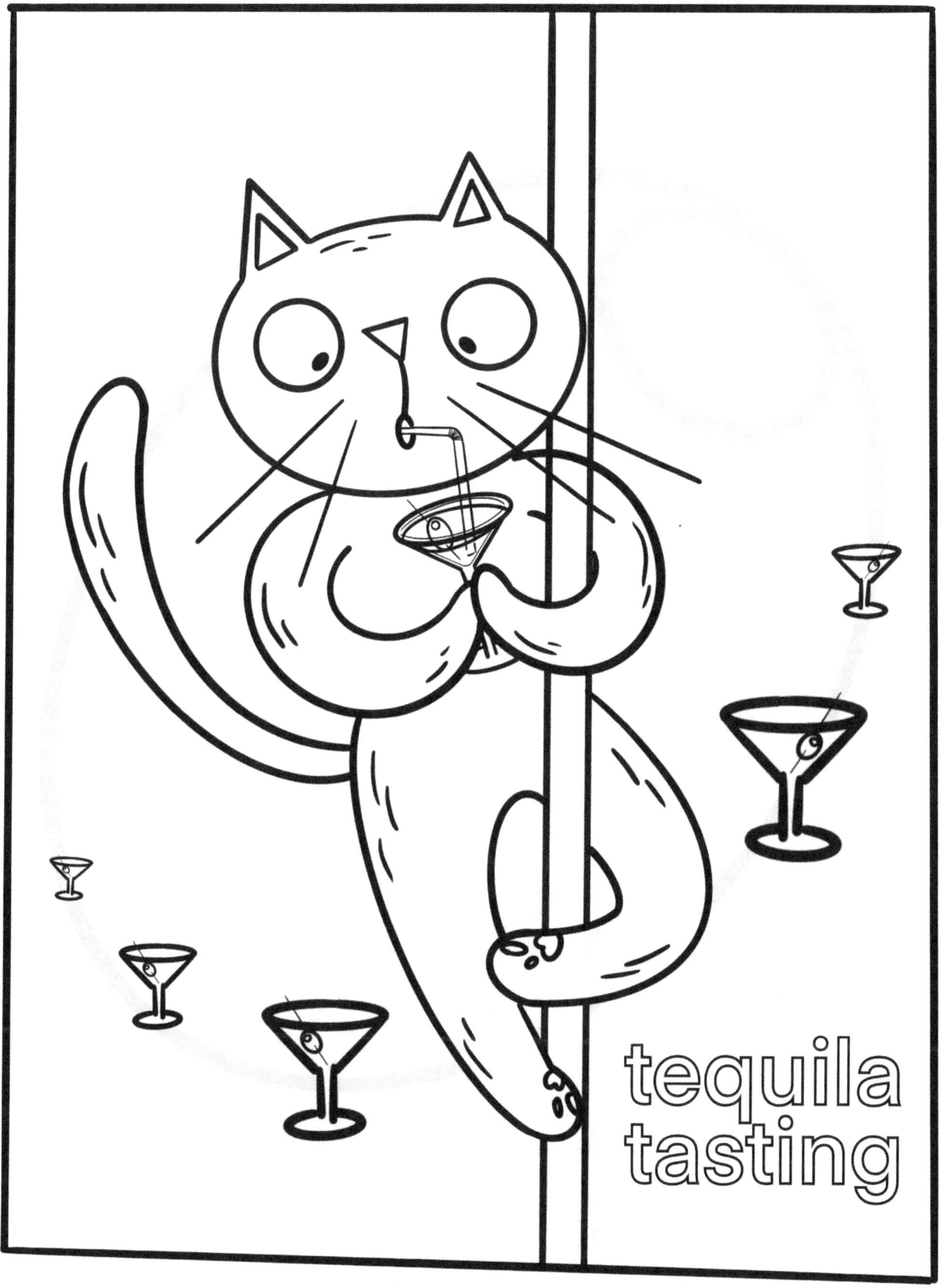
tequila
tasting

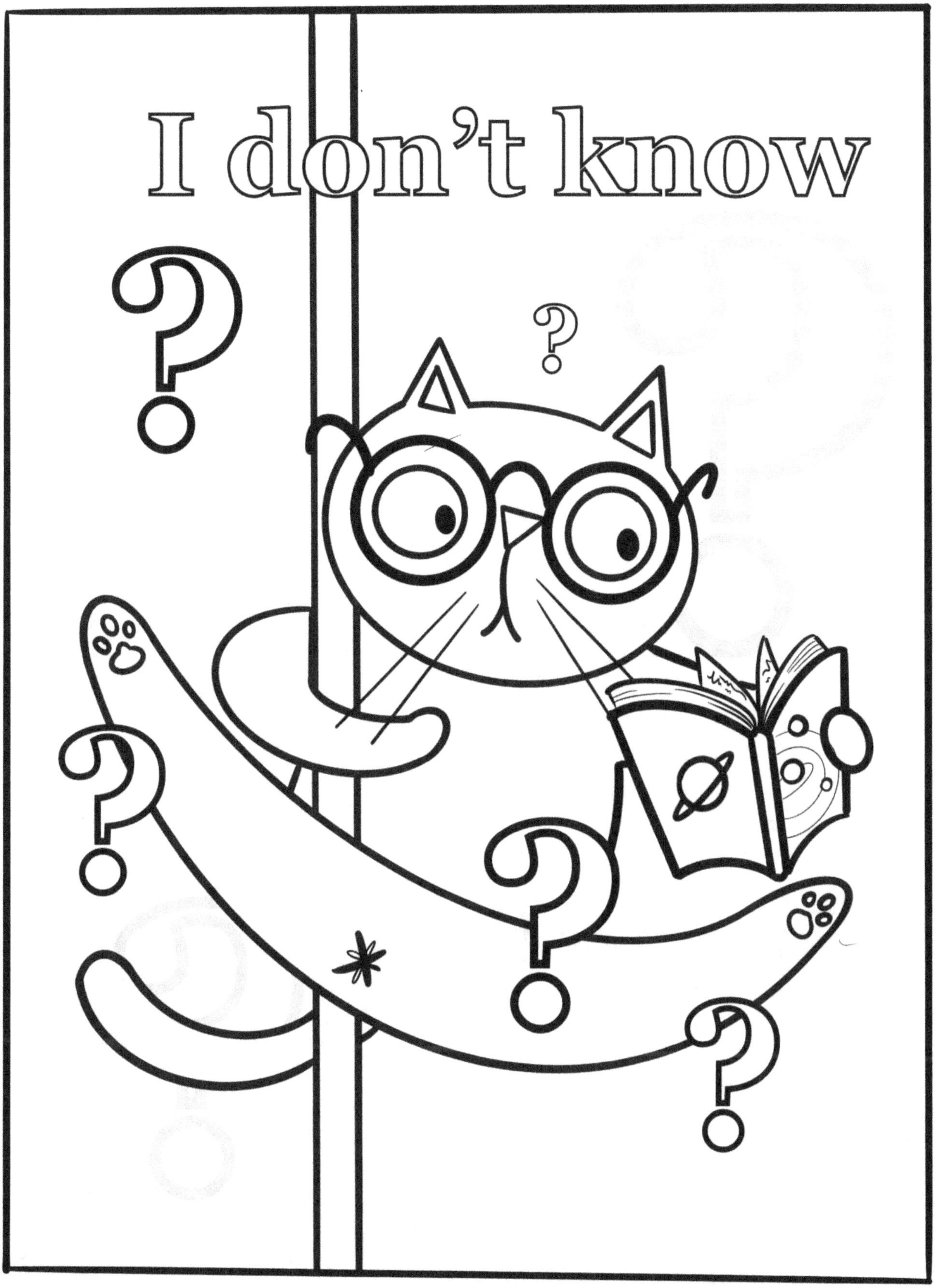
I don't know

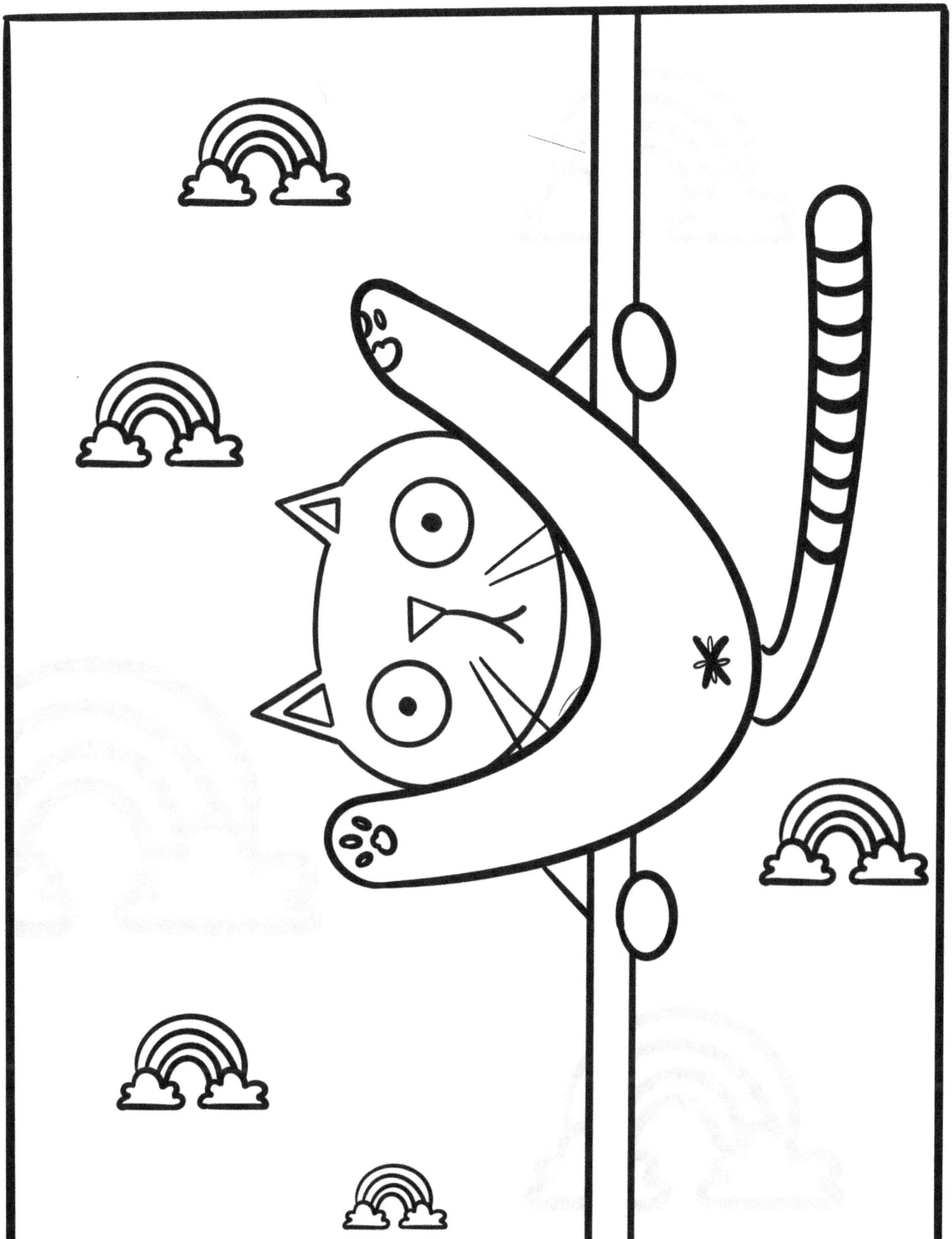

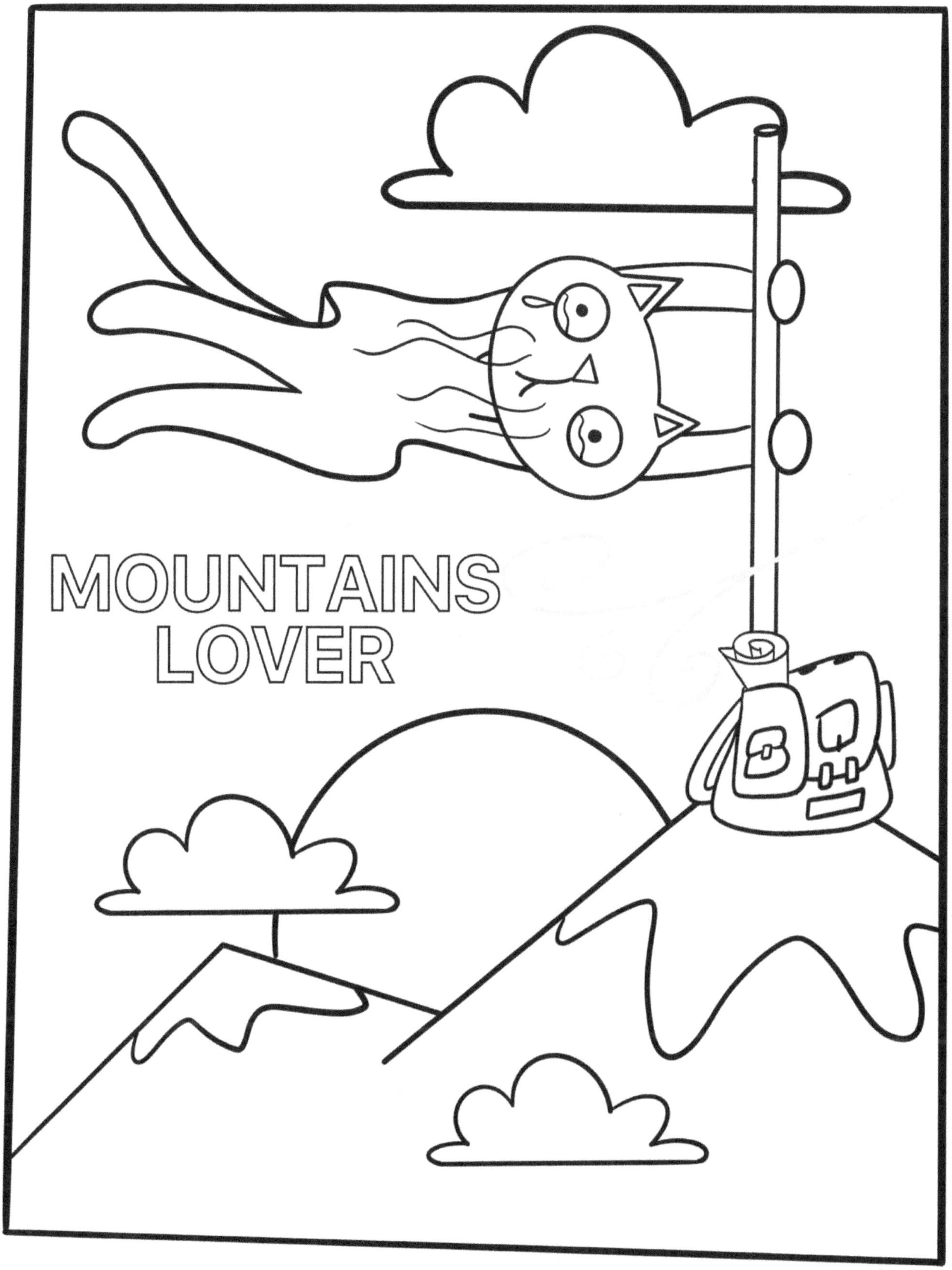
MOUNTAINS
LOVER

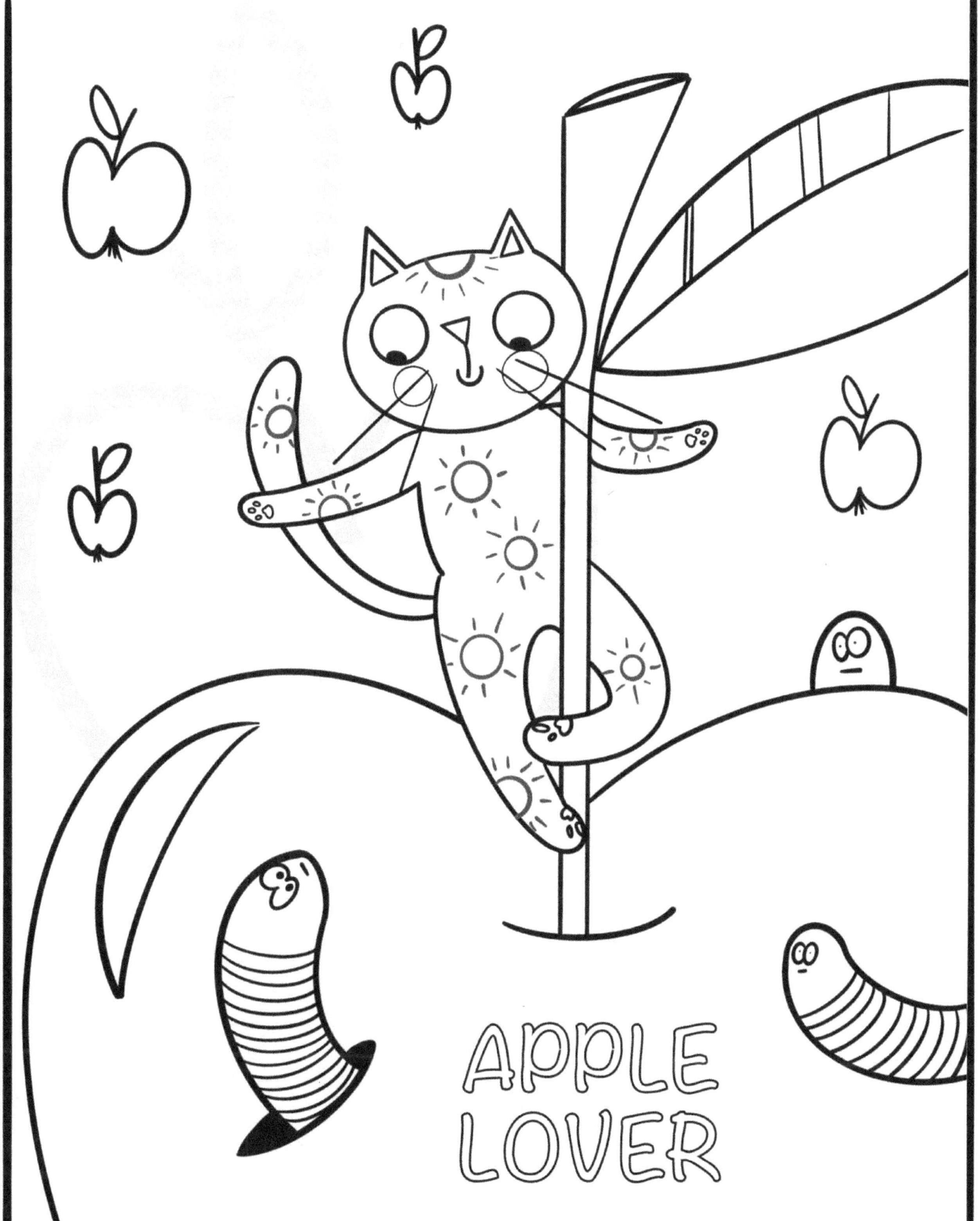
APPLE
LOVER

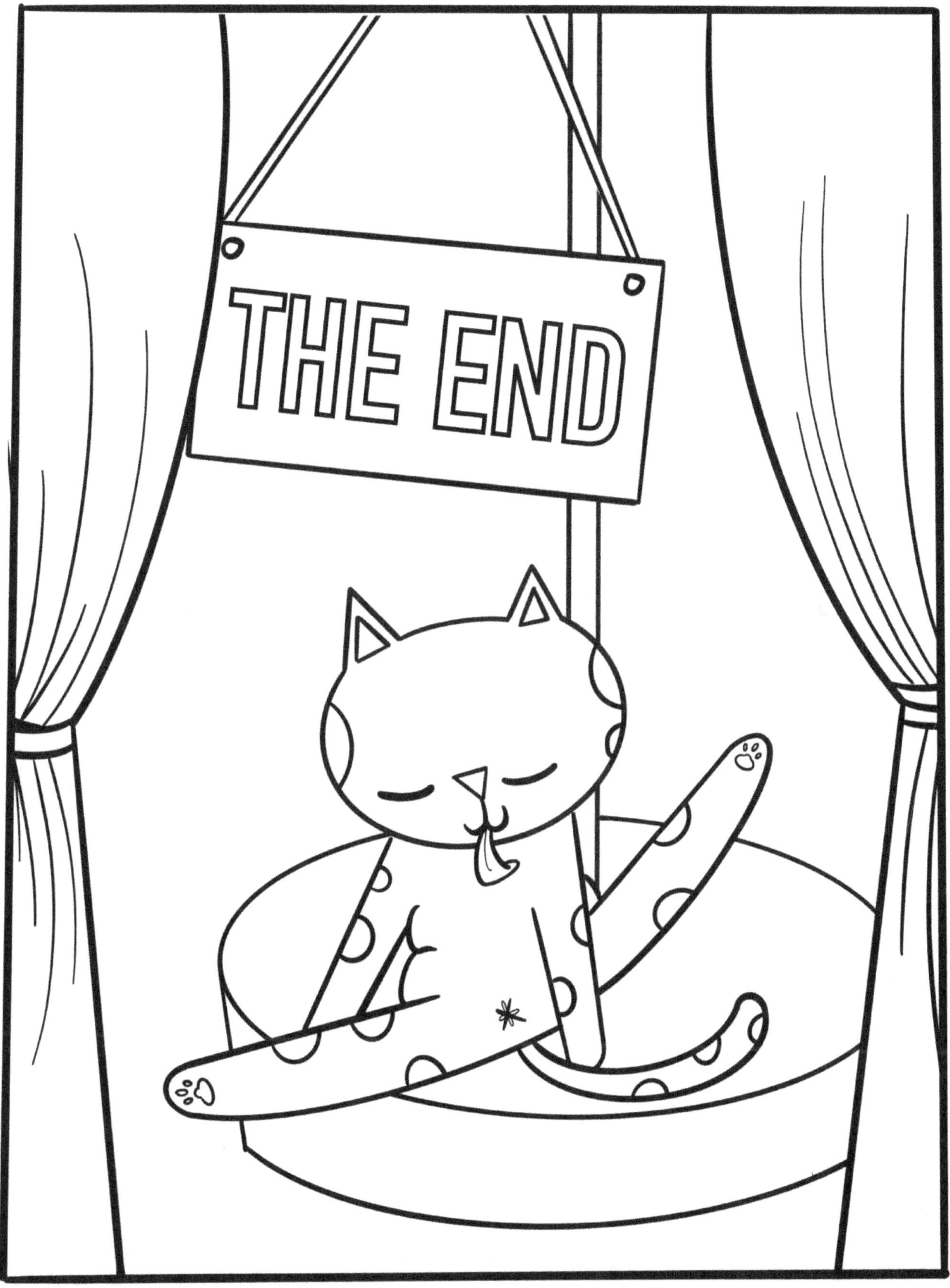
THE END

www.ingramcontent.com/pod-product-compliance
Lightning Source LLC
Chambersburg PA
CBHW082150230526
45467CB00043B/2768
* 9 7 9 8 3 7 9 1 8 0 3 0 0 *